ENTERTAINING AND EDUCATING YOUNG CHILDREN

Robyn Gee

Designed by Kim Blundell

Illustrated by Sue Stitt, Kim Blundell
and Jan Nesbitt

Cover design and illustration by Amanda Barlow

Special consultants: Hank Williams, Ginny Laight, Lesley Lees
and Jean Cook.

Contents

With thanks to: Hilary Abercrombie, Rosalind Barton, Zena Barton, Larraine Biscombe, Pam Blackman, Sarah Bokaie, Diane Brendling, Sheena Collins, Anne Constable, Janet Cooper, Judith Cross, Lucy Delacombe, Jean Eley, Sue Gross, Janet Gupta, Hilary Hammond, Mavis Midgley, Sally Molson, Wendy Morton, Sharon Mowes, Mandy Parker, Pauline Parker, Irene Pryce, Jill Smith, Gillian Styman, Susan Turner, Janice Whatley, Jackie Wisdom, Hilary Worthington, Valery Wright

ABOUT THIS BOOK

In this book you will find lots of ideas to help you entertain young children between the ages of about 2½ and 5 and to help you enjoy the time you spend with them.

The importance of play in the education of young children is now much more widely appreciated than it used to be. Children learn more and at greater speed during the pre-school years than at any other time in their lives. Much research has been done into exactly how and what they learn through play but it is not always obvious to the non-expert how certain types of play contribute to the learning process. The introduction to each topic in this book gives you a brief outline of the learning value of the activities.

Children will play, provided they are not actually prevented from doing so, whether or not they have help from adults but there is no doubt that the learning quality of their play can be greatly influenced by the adults around them. Adults can provide materials, suggest directions, give advice and encouragement and open the door to new activities.

The emphasis in this book is on activities for adults and children to share together.

The selection of activities has been limited to those that require comparatively little preparation or special equipment. The instructions are addressed to adults but the illustrations may fuel children too with ideas. No precise guidelines have been given on the suitable age for each activity, as this depends so much on the individual child but the degree of adult participation will need to vary subtly according to age and ability level. Adults have to strike a delicate balance between helping and interfering. Try to leave as much room as possible for children to discover things for themselves.

There are also suggestions for how to keep children busy while you get on with the many other things you necessarily have to do as a parent.

It is important to remember not to force an activity in an attempt to make a child learn. Play activities should be enjoyable. Follow a child's apparent interests and accept the way she chooses to do things. The process of actively doing something is much more valuable than the result achieved. Remember too to give encouragement and approval.

DRAWING AND COLOURING

Most children progress by the same stages when they are learning to draw but the age at which they reach each stage varies considerably.

By the age of three, a child can usually hold a pencil between his first two fingers and thumb and use it with good control. It is usually clear by now whether he is right- or left-handed. He begins to want to draw, rather than just scribbling, although the finished drawing is unlikely to be recognizable. Children usually start by drawing "people" – heads with limbs and other features coming straight out of the head.

From about four onwards, a child's drawings start to have more detail. People now have heads, legs, arms and fingers, but their bodies are often achieved by shrinking the head and lengthening the legs. A child may decide what to draw before he starts. This is a major step forward from drawing something first and then stating what it is.

From five, pictures containing several different items are produced and there is often an indication of background such as sky. Children can now colour within outlines.

Making marks on paper is the basis of learning to write and gives practice in controlling hand muscles and co-ordinating hand and eye. Drawing and colouring provide opportunities for learning about colours and shapes as well as stimulating children's powers of observation, imagination and communication. They can also give the sense of achievement and self-esteem common to all forms of creativity.

4

Ideas for cheap paper
- ★ Rolls of drawer or wall lining paper
- ★ Back of left-over wallpaper
- ★ Used envelopes opened out
- ★ Wrapping paper from parcels
- ★ Cereal packets cut up
- ★ Inserts from new shirts
- ★ Sugar paper – the cheapest paper to buy from art shops.

It is worth asking local offices if they have any scrap paper. Most throw away masses, especially computer paper that has only been used on one side.

Types of pencil and crayon
- ★ Wax crayons
- ★ Ordinary crayons
- ★ Ordinary lead pencils. Teach your child not to suck them.
- ★ Felt tip pens and magic markers. Buy non-toxic, impermanent ones which will not leave stains on clothes. Teach your child to put the tops back on.
- ★ Plastic crayons
- ★ Charcoal

Chalk and blackboards.
Ordinary chalk is very messy so it is best to buy dustless.
You can buy blackboard paint in hardware stores and paint it on to a wall or piece of hardboard to make a blackboard surface.

Magic slates. These have a built-in erasing device. They are usually quite cheap and do not last long but are excellent for journeys, odd moments during outings and when your child is ill in bed.

Things to do

Stencils and templates

You can buy these or make them quite simply yourself by cutting shapes out of card.

Squiggles and swirls.

Once your child has grasped the idea of colouring in shapes, try drawing swirly lines all over the paper and letting him colour in the holes.

Outlines.

It may help to get an older child started on drawing if you do an outline for him to make into something. If this works, you can turn it into a game and take it in turn to draw outlines for each other, perhaps with your eyes closed.

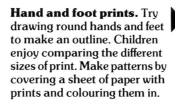

Colouring books.

Though these are often criticized on the grounds that they stifle creativity, there is no evidence for this. Used occasionally, they can give a lot of satisfaction and enjoyment to young children. So too can books of dot-to-dot pictures and simple puzzles.

Hand and foot prints.

Try drawing round hands and feet to make an outline. Children enjoy comparing the different sizes of print. Make patterns by covering a sheet of paper with prints and colouring them in.

Body prints.

If you have a large enough piece of paper (lining paper is ideal) you can get your child to lie down on it and draw his outline. He can then put in features and clothes and colour it in.

Tracing, carbon and graph paper.

These help to ring the changes. Kitchen greaseproof paper can be used as tracing paper. Carbon paper is fun but rather messy. Graph paper can be good for making patterns.

Rubbings.

Cover objects with thin, plain paper (greaseproof is best) and rub with a wax crayon or soft pencil. Try any firm, textured objects such as coins, keys, patterned floor or wall tiles, shoe soles or bark.

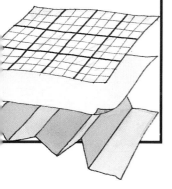

Patterns.

Make simple patterns for children to copy, using some of the marks shown here.

5

PAINTING AND PRINTING

When they first start painting, children need to experiment with the feel of the paint and the way it behaves. Your child may just make a few tentative marks on the painting surface or cover it completely in a single colour. You will have to judge carefully how much help to give. If she is happy with what she is doing, let her carry on. The "doing" is the important part so don't look for results at first.

For a painting session to work, you both need to be relaxed. Get organized before you start so that you do not have to worry about the mess painting will make. It can take half an hour to get everything ready and as long to clear up again so try to ensure your child does not lose interest in painting after only a few minutes by having some suggestions ready. For example, she could start by covering the paper with blobs of colour, then do some stripes before moving on to painting objects such as people or houses.

Materials

Paints. Choose powder paints or liquid poster paints. Paint boxes with hard little blocks of paint are not very satisfactory for young children.

★ Poster paint is more convenient, thicker and more expensive than powder paint.
★ Powder paint is cheaper, needs mixing with water and is not so thick. You can thicken it by mixing it with wallpaper paste (non-fungicidal), flour and water paste, a PVA glue or soapflakes.

If you mix a little washing up liquid into the paint, it will wash off furniture and clothes more easily.

To start with, two colours of paint, or just one, are enough. Later, if you have red, yellow, blue, white and black, you can mix most other colours from them.

Pots and palettes. You need a pot for each colour of paint and at least one pot for water to wash brushes in. It is also useful to have pots or a surface for mixing different coloured paints together.

Use any container that will not be knocked over too easily. Margarine tubs and large plastic ice cream tubs are good. Yoghurt pots are rather unstable. You can also buy special non-spill paint pots from toyshops.

Old bun tins and plastic egg boxes make good mixing palettes.

Paper. See page 4 for ideas for cheap paper. Many children are quite happy to paint on newspaper to start with.

Brushes. Buy fairly flat ones with short handles. A small decorator's brush works quite well. You could also supply other means of applying paint such as cotton wool swabs or pieces of sponge.

Board or easel. You need some way of holding the paper so it does not move under the brush. The simplest way is to attach it to a piece of hardboard or plywood with tape, bulldog clips or clothes-pegs. Easels are useful but quite expensive to buy.

Protective covering. If you have to worry about where the paint is going, it will take a lot of the fun out of painting sessions, so it is worth providing good protection for clothes, floor and table-tops.

For overalls you can use an old shirt worn back to front with the sleeves cut down; a plastic mac cut down to size; or a carrier bag with the bottom cut out and the handles as shoulder straps.

For table and floor covering use thick layers of newspaper, plastic tablecloths or cheap polythene sheeting bought from a garden centre.

Painting ideas

Finger painting

The easiest way to start a child finger painting is to cover a surface with thick paint and let him draw in it with his fingers.

Old tea trays and plastic-coated boards and worktops make good painting surfaces. If you use paper it has to be fairly thick.

The paint also needs to be thick. You can buy specially thick poster paints called finger paints, or use powder paints or food colouring to colour a thick paste. For the paste use wallpaper glue (non-fungicidal), or flour and water, or one of the recipes below:

1 Mix together ½ cup soapflakes*
                 ½ cup cold water starch
                 ¾ cup cold water

        or

2 Dissolve 1 cup cornflour in a little water
   Add 1 litre (2 pints) boiling water
   Boil until thick
   Take off heat
   Beat in 1 cup soapflakes*

Some children do not like getting their hands dirty at first. Let your child use something to draw with or try drawing a simple picture and get her to put in dots with her fingers.

Drip painting.
Make the paint quite thin and runny. Show your child how to put a blob of paint on the paper and roll it around to make a pattern.

Blow painting. Put blobs of runny paint on the paper and use a straw to blow it into different shapes.

Spray painting. Dip a toothbrush into runny paint and then run your finger over it to send a spray of paint on to the paper. Try making shapes on the paper by placing objects on it before you spray.

Invisible pictures.
Use a white candle to draw an invisible picture on a sheet of paper. Then cover the paper with thin paint and the picture will appear.

Rainbows. Use a brush to cover an entire sheet of paper with water, then paint in arches of different colours with a slight gap between them. Watch the arches slowly blend into each other to make a rainbow.

Make sure you use real soapflakes and not detergent.

7

Printing ideas

Children can have a lot of fun experimenting with different ways of printing. This may make fewer demands on the imagination than "free expression" painting but they can get some satisfying results nevertheless. Here are some ideas.

Blob prints. To make blob prints, fold a piece of paper in half, then open it and drop big blobs of runny paint on to one half of the paper near the fold. Fold the clean half over and press hard before opening it up again.

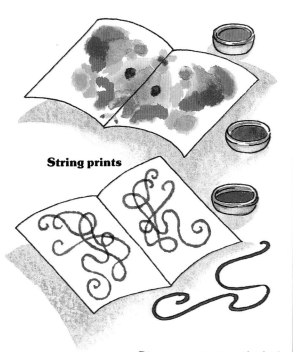

String prints

Dip some string into thickish paint, making sure it gets well covered. Drop it on to one side of a sheet of paper with a fold in it. Fold the other side over and press hard before opening it up.

Try leaving one end of the string hanging over the edge of the paper. Then pull the string out while folding and pressing the paper. Repeat with different colours to get the effect above.

Vegetable prints. Various vegetables dipped in paint make interesting prints.

Carrot

Leek

To make potato prints, cut a potato in half and carve shapes in the cut surface.

Hand and foot prints. Put fairly thick paint on to an old tray or unbreakable plate and let your child print in it with different parts of his hands and feet.

Side of finger

Whole hand

Fingertips

Side of thumb

Side of fist

Knuckles

Heel

Toes

Whole foot

Using a screen. Use a paper doily or cut shapes through both thicknesses of a folded piece of paper to make a screen. Place the screen on top of another piece of paper and spread paint over it with a brush or sponge.

You can also try laying the screen over a tray of paint and pressing a clean sheet of paper over the top.

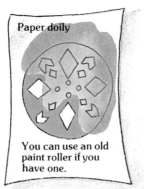

Paper doily

You can use an old paint roller if you have one.

Other things to try

The choice of objects to print with is almost limitless. Here are just a few suggestions.

End of cardboard tube

Cotton reel

Thimble

Straw

Screw

Balloon

Sponge

Clothes-peg

Pieces of polystyrene packing

Pasta

Corrugated card

Comb

Using blocks. You can make printing blocks quite simply by cutting designs into blocks of plasticine, foam rubber or polystyrene (the type used for packing fragile objects).

Polystyrene tile

Plasticine

Cotton reel

Thick card

Alternatively, cut shapes out of cardboard and glue them to blocks so children can hold them easily. Cotton reels, toy bricks and match-boxes all make good blocks.

Printed decorations. Make wrapping paper or a poster by printing a design all over a sheet of paper. For parties, print on to tablecloths, napkins, mats, cups and hats made of plain paper.

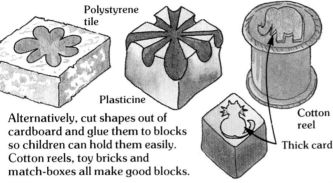

Printing tips and hints

★ The secret of making good prints is to have the paint the right thickness. You may need to experiment with this, using flour as a thickener and water as a thinner.

★ Thick, non-shiny paper works best. Putting a thick wad of newspaper under the paper helps to get clear prints.

★ Use a brush to put the paint on to the printing object or dip it into the paint. It may be easier to use a piece of thick cloth, sponge or foam rubber.

★ It is handy to have somewhere to dry prints. You could rig up a string drying line and hang them up with clothes-pegs.

★ To make a change, try printing in white and light colours on to black paper.

CUTTING AND STICKING

There is a huge range of different materials that can be used for cutting and sticking. As well as developing children's hand control, cutting and sticking stimulates their imagination and creativity, whether they are working out how best to use the materials they have, or are spotting new ones that they could use. It is also a good way of making cards and presents for people.

Learning to use scissors

This is a fairly difficult skill to master and children should always be supervised when using scissors. These should be sharp enough to cut easily but have rounded ends. "Safety" scissors, which have a plastic coating over the blades, are a good idea. They are often made in animal shapes.

Children usually start by holding the scissors in both hands and find straight lines easiest to cut. Try drawing a pencil line on the paper for your child to follow. Then, once she can follow straight lines, start her on curves and circles. Old newspaper is useful for practising on.

If your child has difficulty in using scissors, there are lots of things she can make by tearing paper instead of cutting.

Types of glue

Be careful when choosing glue. Never give your child a glue which gives off vapours and don't use glues which say they give "instant bonding".
★ Liquid glues are quite adequate for sticking paper to paper.
★ Glue sticks are also good for gluing paper to paper and for other lightweight materials.
★ PVA (polyvinyl acetate) glue is strong and good for sticking heavier materials. It is white but goes transparent when dry.
★ Flour and water paste can be used if you have no proper glue. Mix together flour and water to make a smooth paste. Bring to the boil and simmer for a few moments.
★ Wallpaper paste is good for sticking paper, but be sure to use a non-fungicidal type.

Things to cut and stick

All the things listed below could come in useful but you will only need a small selection at a time, say up to six things.

Paper and card
Old newspapers
Tissue paper
Crêpe paper
Scraps of wallpaper
Used wrapping paper
Old birthday and Christmas cards
Old magazines
Old catalogues and leaflets
Gummed paper
Gummed paper shapes
Thick paper or card (for the base for collage pictures)

Things from the kitchen
Kitchen foil
Drinking straws
Doilies
Seeds (melon, marrow, sunflower, for example)
Egg shells (wash and leave to dry, then crush.)
Egg boxes
Foil tops and wrappers
Pasta
Lentils
Beans
Rice
Cereal
Salt
Spices
Herbs
Tea
Coffee
Cocoa

Miscellaneous
Cotton wool
Glitter (Use with care.)

Sewing materials
Wool
Embroidery silk
Ribbon
Scraps of fabric

Things from out-of-doors
Twigs
Feathers
Small shells
Pressed flowers and grasses
Wood-shavings
Sawdust
Sand (Light-coloured sand can be coloured. Put a little dry sand into an old jam jar, add a few drops of food colouring and shake well. Then spread the sand on a sheet of paper to dry.)

Ideas for things to make

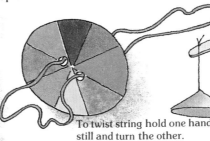

Dancing dolls. Make several concertina-style folds in a piece of paper. Cut out a figure with arms outstretched to the edges of the paper. Unfold and you have a row of people.

Don't cut here.

Paper snowflakes. Cut a circle out of thin white paper and fold it in half three times. Snip little pieces from the sides and open out.

To twist string hold one hand still and turn the other.

Mosaics. Tear or cut coloured paper or pictures from magazines into small bits. Stick them on a piece of paper to make a mosaic, or as decoration on boxes or tins.

Whizzer. Cut a circle out of card and colour it in several colours. Make two holes in the centre, thread string through and tie it. Twist the string, then pull outwards to make the circle whizz round.

Mobiles. Cut shapes out of coloured card, tie or stick them to pieces of thread and hang them from a coat-hanger to move gently in a draught.

Fish collage. Draw or cut out the shape of a fish and glue on silver milk bottle tops to give the effect of scales. Strips of blue and green tissue paper make a good sea background.

Princess collage. Draw or cut out a princess with a large ball gown. Decorate the gown with scraps of material, tissue paper or foil.

Other collage ideas
Ideas for collage are limitless. Here are a few more suggestions:

Tissue paper vase of flowers
Drinking straw hedgehog
Egg-shell tortoise
Egg-box monster
Fluffy chicken (use yellow cotton wool)
Stained glass window (use cellophane or tissue paper)
Night-time scene (use silver foil on black background)

You could also try copying a simple picture from a book, or doing a portrait of a teddy, favourite animal or member of the family.

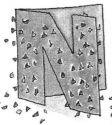

Cut-out cards. Make cards for friends by folding paper in half and cutting out the initial letter of their name or their age.

Pop-up cards. Fold a piece of paper in half and cut out a shape, then glue it by its edges across the centre of a card.

11

MODELLING AND BUILDING

Modelling and building give children the opportunity to learn about different materials and the way they behave. It is both a tactile and a creative activity, giving scope to the imagination and building self-confidence. It can even be the first step towards learning to appreciate the visual arts such as sculpture. On a more commonplace level, it is soothing and relaxing.

Making playdough

You can buy playdough but it is quite simple and a good deal cheaper to make it. Plasticine and other ready-made clays tend to be a bit too stiff for this age group.

Basic playdough. Flour and water are the basic ingredients. Salt helps to preserve it and keep it moist, but makes it a little brittle. Oil helps to counteract this, making it glossy and pliable. You need approximately two measures of flour for every one of salt and water.

> 2 cups plain flour
> 1 cup salt
> 1 cup cold water
> 1 tablespoon oil

Adding colour. Use food colouring or paint. For a smooth, even colour, mix the colouring with the water before it is added to the flour and salt; for a streaky, marbled effect, knead it straight into the dough.

Adding smells. To ring the changes try adding one of the following: peppermint essence, ginger, cinnamon or rosewater. Don't do this for smaller children as it may increase the temptation to eat the dough.

Stretchy playdough. Instead of plain flour mix self-raising flour with water to make a dough that is puffy and stretchy but does not last very long.

Long-lasting playdough. By adding cream of tartar to the recipe and cooking the mixture you can make a dough that lasts well and has a lovely texture.

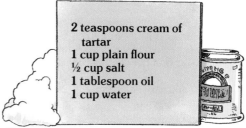

> 2 teaspoons cream of tartar
> 1 cup plain flour
> ½ cup salt
> 1 tablespoon oil
> 1 cup water

Mix to form a smooth paste. Put in a saucepan and cook slowly, until the dough comes away from the side of the pan and forms a ball. When it is cool enough, take the dough out of the pan and knead for three to four minutes. Put the pan to soak immediately.

Making things from junk

Collecting junk. Start by collecting boxes (cereal and tea packets, shoe boxes, match-boxes, juice containers), tubes (paper towel and toilet roll, washing up liquid bottles, herb pots) and tubs (margarine, ice-cream and yoghurt cartons). You will soon develop an eye for other things that will come in handy.

Building blocks. Stuff the boxes, tubes and tubs with newspaper and tape the ends closed. To paint them mix up some powder paints and add a little washing up liquid to make the paint spread more easily.

Fixing and sticking. The following can all be used to help to construct things from boxes, tubes and tubs: ordinary paper clips, split-pin paper clips, hair grips, rubber bands, staples, sticky tape, pieces of string, pipe cleaners, PVA glue. Here are some things you could make.

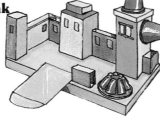

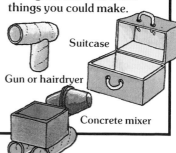

Suitcase

Gun or hairdryer

Concrete mixer

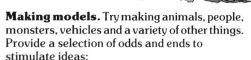

Playing with playdough

This is not necessarily a messy activity, but don't play over a carpet or rug as bits can easily get trodden in. Formica, plastic tablecloths or large trays make the best work surfaces.

Squeezing, pinching and punching. When they are first introduced to playdough, children are often happy simply to handle it and squash it about, without trying to make anything. Let them explore its possibilities by themselves for a while.

Play cooking. It is very useful to have some playdough handy for when you want to cook without children joining in. Provide some implements so that they can imitate what they see:
Rolling pin (You can make one out of a small piece of dowelling or broom handle.)
Shape cutters
Plastic knives
Spatula
Variety of containers and their lids (to act as bowls, plates and pans)

Making models. Try making animals, people, monsters, vehicles and a variety of other things. Provide a selection of odds and ends to stimulate ideas:

Pebbles	Bottle caps
Used matches	Buttons
Drinking straws (cut into pieces)	Wool
	String
Lolly sticks	Rubbish bag ties

Sculpting. Let a lump of playdough go a bit dry and carve it with plastic knives or used matches.

Making things to keep. To make models last, bake them in a fairly hot oven until they go hard (about 10 to 20 minutes depending on size). When cool they can be painted with poster paints.
Try making pretend food for dolls and teddies, play money for shops, and jewellery for dressing up (see page 29).

Storing playdough

Playdough dries out when exposed to air so if you want it to last, store it in an airtight container, such as a plastic bag or box, and keep it in the fridge. Kept like this, the basic playdough will last for a week or two and the long-lasting dough for several months. If it gets left out accidentally and starts going dry and crumbly, you may be able to rescue it with a little water and oil.

Woodwork

Children can get a lot out of working with real tools and wood at a surprisingly early age. You need to supervise them carefully and show them how to use each tool properly.

Hammer, nails and wood. Hammering nails into wood can be very absorbing. Strength and aim are not good at first, so provide a strong, light hammer, nails with large heads and soft wood.

Glue and paint. To stick pieces of wood together, use PVA glue. To paint, use powder or poster paint with some PVA glue mixed in.

Saws and clamps. Some four and five-year-olds can use saws very competently. A saw needs to be strong and sharp – a tenon or junior hacksaw is best. The wood must be held in a vice or G-clamp.

Screws and screwdrivers. Use a gimlet, bradawl or drill to make holes in a piece of wood. The child can then practise screwing in screws.

Sandpaper, files and planes. Some children really enjoy simply working on a piece of wood to make it smooth.

BOOKS, PICTURES AND STORIES

It is never too early to introduce your child to books, both for the enjoyment they provide and for their learning value. Looking at books together is also a valuable shared experience which can strengthen the emotional links between you. Use books as often as possible but never force them on a child who would clearly prefer to be doing something else.

Using books helps to develop children's powers of observation and their ability to listen. It improves their skill at talking and encourages the desire to communicate. Use of language is closely linked with the ability to think. Books also stimulate the imagination and encourage emotional development as the child begins to appreciate how other people feel. They extend his knowledge of the world by introducing him to new situations and deepening his understanding of those he has already experienced.

If a child is used to books and enjoys them, he is more likely to want to learn to read. Looking at books early teaches him valuable pre-reading skills, such as an awareness of detail and the knack of moving his eyes from left to right.

A child's attitude to books is conditioned by his parents'. If he sees that you enjoy reading and refer to books for information, he is likely to think of books as enjoyable.

Choosing and using books

Which books? Introduce your child to as great a variety as possible: books with different types of illustration, some detailed, some simple, for example; books with different subject matter such as stories, information or rhymes; books of different size, shape and length. Be guided by your own taste and your child's enthusiasms. Some books will be mainly for looking at and talking about; others will be for reading.

Libraries. Borrowing books from the library is the best way of providing your child with variety and allowing him to develop his taste without any expense. There is usually a children's librarian who can advise you which books to choose. Many libraries organize story-telling sessions to encourage children's interest in books.

Bookshops. Try to find a bookshop that encourages browsing, can give you advice and has facilities for children, such as a special reading corner. Second-hand bookshops and jumble sales can be good places for buying picture books cheaply.

Book clubs and book parties. Book clubs sell books at reduced prices, usually in return for a promise that you will buy a certain number of books a year. They send you information about current offers, including the age range each book is suitable for, and you order by post.

Book parties are held in people's homes and provide a good opportunity to look at books and discuss them with others before you buy them.

Storytime. It is a good idea to have a certain time each day that is specially devoted to books, perhaps just before bedtime. The attention you give your child, the physical closeness, warmth and feeling of security will all contribute to his enjoyment of books.

Reading aloud. If you start by talking through picture books with your child, reading stories will follow naturally. Always read slowly and clearly, and try to change expression and pace to hold his interest. You can alter or shorten the text if you think it is too hard but remember that stories are a good opportunity for children to learn new words.

Fathers and reading. It is important for fathers to make a special effort to read and to be seen reading. Far more boys than girls are poor readers. The reason for this is thought to be that most teachers of young children are female and mothers read to their children more than fathers, so boys can get the impression that men do not care about books.

Book corners. It is a good idea to have a small, cosy corner somewhere in the house that is specially for books. This will encourage your child to look at books by himself.

Protecting books. Teach your child to treat books with respect and not tear them, write in them or throw them around but try not to be too protective of them. You can always cover them with clear, self-adhesive plastic.

Books and television. Don't make books compete with television for your child's attention by having the television on in the background while you are reading together. Children who otherwise show little interest in books may start to enjoy them by looking at books based on their favourite programmes. Don't let television become a substitute for books.

Making your own books

Helping your child to make his own book is a good way of encouraging a liking for books.

Buy a scrapbook or notebook, or fold large sheets of paper in half, punch two holes along the fold and thread string, wool or ribbon through them.

A book about me. Include drawings or photographs of family, friends, pets, toys, bedroom, favourite things, holidays, birthday, favourite foods.

Favourite topics. Collect pictures from old magazines on favourite topics such as cars, animals or food.

Shape and colours. Collect pictures of different shaped objects and have a page for each shape. Do the same for colours.

Stories. If your child is starting to show an interest in writing, help him to make up a story and write down what he dictates. He can then illustrate the story.

Making up stories

You do not need a special talent or brilliant imagination to make up stories that your child will enjoy. A photograph or picture may help to start you off. You can even get your child's assistance by asking "What do you think happened next?" and building his answers into the story.

Most children love thinly disguised stories about themselves and also like stories about what their parents did when they were small. The tiniest incidents soon get elaborated on and become favourite family tales.

If you turn a story into a serial to give you time to make up the next episode, remember always to leave it at an exciting part.

FUN WITH WORDS AND LETTERS

Playing games which involve recognizing letters of the alphabet and whole words is something most small children will enjoy if it is approached in the right way. It can also form the basis of learning to read and write. It is unwise, though, to place too much emphasis on the "learning to read" aspect of the games. If this starts to override the play element, it can do more harm than good.

When are children ready for these games?

They are ready when they show an interest if you point out words and letters on signs and in books, or write things for them. Seeing their own name written down usually interests them at this stage and the first letter of their name is usually the first they recognize. They will be more interested if they enjoy being read to and have some understanding of the usefulness of reading. They must have a well-developed awareness of detail to be able to distinguish the differences between letter shapes. Their concentration and memory must also be sufficiently developed. These skills of memory, concentration and visual awareness form an important part of what are often termed the "pre-reading skills".

Capital letters and small letters

Many capital letters bear little relation in shape to their small (lower case) equivalents, so learning both sets is almost like learning two alphabets. To make it easier, children are usually taught only small letters to start with. However, use capitals where common sense suggests it, such as for the first letters of names.

Letter sounds and letter names

Most experts feel it is better to tell children the letter sounds rather than the letter names – "kuh" rather than "see" for "c" – as it makes it easier for them to join the letters up into words later on. However, letters sounded in isolation sound very different from the way they are pronounced in a word and it is debatable whether it makes a great deal of difference.

Teaching methods and reading schemes

Parents often worry that starting to teach their children to read may actually confuse them when they go to school. This only happens in rare cases where a school sticks very rigidly to an unusual reading method.

The "phonic" method involves recognizing letters and letter sounds and building up words from them. The "look and say" method involves learning to recognize whole words and so having the satisfaction of being able to read sentences earlier. Most schools use a combination of these methods and it is best to play games that involve recognition of whole words as well as single letters.

How to form the letters of the alphabet

It is important when writing letters for children, or teaching them how to write, that you know how to form each letter correctly yourself. This is shown below.

abcdefghijklmn
opqrstuvwxyz

Learning to recognize words

A word's overall shape is composed of its length and the arrangement of the letters' up and down "tails" (ascenders and descenders). It is as easy to learn to recognize whole word shapes as it is to recognize words from their individual letters, although initial letters may provide a clue to what the word is.

Word cards

These are pieces of card, usually about the size of a postcard, with one word written on each. They are used to help children learn to recognize words and are very simple to make. It is best if you start with your child's name and then move on to people and things she knows well. Introduce the cards one at a time, waiting until she knows each word before going on to the next. Once she can recognize several cards, there are all sorts of games you can play – below are some ideas. You could also make picture cards to match each word card.

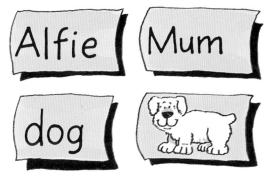

Find the pair. Use pairs of words or words and pictures. Start by having the cards turned face up to look for pairs. Move on to having them all face down except one and take it in turns to turn over a card until you find its pair. Then take it in turns to turn over two cards at once, aiming to find a matching pair.

Snap. Write each word on several cards. You can also add pictures to make it easier. Each have a pile and take it in turns to turn over a card. First one to spot a pair shouts "Snap".

Word bingo. Have large cards divided into squares. Write a word, or stick or draw a picture, in each square. Take it in turns to pick up a word card. If it matches a word or picture on your large card, place it on top of it. The first to cover a complete row or, if you prefer, the whole card, is the winner.

Action cards. Write an action word such as "jump", "sit", "run" on each card. The game involves picking out a card and doing the action written on it as quickly as possible. You could also write the names of pieces of furniture that have to be touched or rooms that have to be visited.

17

Recognizing letter sounds

It takes a lot of practice for children to be able to recognize letter sounds when they form part of a word. Once your child can recognize one or two letter sounds at the beginning of words, you can try some games.

I spy. "I spy with my little eye something beginning with –." Give additional clues to start with, for example: "It's black, it purrs and it begins with 'kuh'."

Odd one out. Say a number of words, all but one of which begin with the same letter, and see if your child can spot the odd one out. If he gets good at this, try it with last letters.

Rhymes. Playing around with rhymes helps a great deal with recognition of similar sounds. Play rhyming versions of I spy and Odd man out, for example: "Can you see something that rhymes with 'bat'?"

Alphabet scrapbook.
Write a letter at the top of each page of a scrapbook. Concentrating on a few letters at a time, collect pictures of objects that begin with those letters and stick them on the appropriate pages. Write the names of the objects underneath.

Learning to write letters

The manual skill needed to write words develops more slowly than the ability to read them.

Pencils should be held lightly between the thumb and first two fingers about 3cm from the point.

Left-handers should grip even further from the point so that they can see what they are writing. Their paper should be slightly to the left of centre of their bodies and either parallel to the edge of the table or slanted slightly to the right.

Recognizing letter shapes

As well as the 26 small letters, there are 17 new capital letter shapes to be learnt. Over half the letters of the alphabet can become other letters if they are turned over or twisted round and children often find this confusing. Here are some games to help them.

Letter cards. You can use letter cards in the same way as word cards (see page 25). Introduce the letters one at a time, in whatever order you find easiest, but avoid introducing letters of similar shape too close together. Wait until your child knows each new shape before introducing the next one.

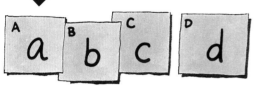

Letter fishing. Put a selection of letter cards in a box or bowl. Your child pulls out one card at a time. If he knows it, he keeps it as part of his catch. If he does not, he puts it on a pile of "ones that got away". At the end the catch is counted. You can make this game more fun by putting a paper clip on each card and fishing with a horseshoe magnet on a string.

Letter building. Cut out a selection of shapes – short, medium and long straight pieces, half circles, hooks and arches. You can play around with these together to see what letters you can make. Give your child a selection of two or three shapes and ask him what letters he can make out of them. You can also have fun making letters out of pipe-cleaners and playdough.

Post a letter. Cut a slot in an empty cereal packet or shoe box. Ask your child if she can find an "m" to send to a monkey, or a "p" to send to a pig and so on with other letters of the alphabet.

Patterns. The formation of letters is based on certain recurring patterns. Copying patterns helps to increase manual control and prepare the way for writing.

Sand or salt tray. Children enjoy writing with their fingers and have more control that way than when using pencils and pens. Writing letters with finger paints is also fun.

Tracing and joining up dotted letters. This is useful because it helps to imprint on a child's mind the feel of writing letters without his having to think too hard about how to form them.

Fill in the first letter. Filling in a letter to complete a word is a useful first step towards writing a whole word.

FUN WITH NUMBERS

1 2 3 4

Numbers, like letters, can provide a lot of entertainment for small children. They first become familiar with the sound of numbers, then begin to understand the concept of them and to recognize them when they are written down. Learning to count requires a great deal of repetition and games are the best way to make the repetition interesting.

Many other activities contribute considerably to mathematical skill later in life. Number play is just a part of this. Matching, sorting and ordering, playing with shapes, and other activities which develop the concepts of position, size and amount are all important too.

The sound of numbers

Children can start to recognize the sound of numbers from a very early age if they hear number songs and rhymes and hear people counting. They may even appear to be able to count by reciting numbers from one to ten but this has very little meaning for them. They then start to notice numbers in everyday speech and to develop some understanding of the context in which they are used.

Five little sparrows sitting in a row.

Numbers all around

Point out numbers that appear in different everyday contexts. This helps children to begin not only to recognize written numbers but to understand that they have a practical use, helping to distinguish one thing or amount from another.

Learning to count

Before learning to count properly, a child needs to understand what teachers refer to as "one-to-one correspondence". This simply means being able to match one object to one other object or person.

Can you find a cup for each animal? We need one for Hippo, one for Monkey and one for Teddy.

You can practise this in all sorts of different contexts, counting the objects once your child starts to get the idea. Laying the table is a good one. Drawing is another.

Can you draw one mouse for each cat to catch?

Can you draw a line between each mouse and each cat?

As you count objects together, touch each one. Don't start by trying to count objects that you cannot touch. Touching helps children to understand that they are counting one thing at a time.

Don't go beyond three until your child has really mastered counting up to three. Then add one more number at a time.

Occasionally mix up the order of the things you are counting to make sure your child does not think a certain object has a certain number.

Things to do

Counting trays. Use an egg carton, a bun tin or a collection of plastic tubs. Write numbers on the bottom of the containers or on bits of paper to put into them. Provide a pile of dried beans or pasta and show your child how to count the appropriate number into each container. Underline 6 and 9 to avoid confusion.

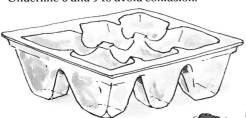

Step, hop, jump. Take it in turns to give instructions to each other, such as "Take three big steps, two tiny hops and one jump". When the player makes a mistake, it is her turn to give instructions to you.

Throwing games. Games which involve throwing a number of objects into a container, such as a waste paper basket, can give good counting practice.

Dice games. You can make games to play with dice quite easily by drawing a course, like the one below, on a piece of paper. Choose objects to move round the course. The dice determines the moves each player makes.

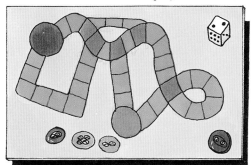

Number cards. Make number cards from pieces of card about the size of large postcards. On one side of each card write a number and on the other draw and colour in the corresponding number of large spots. Some people cut shapes out of gummed paper and stick them on instead. Others sew buttons on.

Lay the cards out, spotted sides up. Ask your child to put them in order or leave one out and see if she can tell which one is missing.

Try making two or more cards for each number but arrange the spots differently on each one. See if your child can match the cards with the same number of spots.

Give your child a pile of counters, buttons or coins. Show her the number written on one card. She then has to give you that number of counters. She can check her answer by placing them on top of the spots on the other side of the card.

Make bingo cards by dividing large sheets of paper into rectangles the same size as your number cards. Write a number in each rectangle. Each person takes a card and if its number appears on their bingo sheet uses it to cover the number up. Continue until someone fills their sheet and shouts "Bingo".

Shopping games. A play shop gives excellent opportunities for counting out money and, later, for adding up different amounts and subtracting to find the right change. Write prices on the goods for sale.

21

LISTENING TO AND MAKING MUSIC

Parents can introduce their children to music in two main ways. First, by making them aware of sound and helping them to learn to listen. Listening is an acquired art that children develop through practice. It is worth helping to develop this skill because it plays such an important part in learning and communication in general and not just in musical activities. Second, they can encourage them to experiment with making sound and using their bodies to respond to it.

You do not need to have musical ability or any knowledge of music to be able to help your child develop an interest in and enjoyment of music. While it is true that musical ability is a natural gift, nearly everyone is capable of getting a great deal out of music, provided they are exposed to it in ways that they enjoy.

Apart from straightforward enjoyment, music can bring other benefits. Children who have learnt to listen to songs, and join in, tend to become more confident in their use of words – speech therapists use musical activities specifically to help children with speech defects. It is also an excellent vehicle for releasing tension and letting off steam.

Choosing music to listen to

Provide plenty of variety in your choice of music for your child to listen to and avoid trying to impose your own musical tastes. Children have a very short attention span when just listening, so choose short pieces. Follow what you know a child enjoys and watch for signs that a piece has caught their attention, however briefly.

Most children prefer music with strong rhythms which suggest movement; band music tends to go down well. If there are words they need to be very clear for a child to understand them when sung. Point out the sounds of individual instruments if they are easy to pick out.

Learning to listen

The first stage in learning to listen is to become aware of as many different sounds as possible. You can encourage this in a variety of ways. Simply pointing out sounds and talking about them is very helpful and provides children with words with which to describe sound. Below is a selection of games which encourage listening.

Listening games

How many sounds? Get children to close eyes, keep still and count the number of sounds they can hear. Works best outside.

What am I doing now? One person closes eyes, the other has to guess what they are doing – things like opening a door, bouncing a ball, turning the pages of a newspaper.

What made the noise? Select three or four objects that make different noises. Listen to the noises. Child closes eyes while you remove one, and then has to work out which one is missing.

Paper sounds. Listen together to the different sounds made by tearing, crumpling or flapping paper. Child has to close eyes and guess which you are doing. Try also using different types of paper – tissue, wrapping, newspaper. Child has to guess which you are using.

Dropping sounds. Choose three different things, such as a coin, a paper clip and a pencil, to drop into a box or tin. Child has to close eyes and guess which is being dropped. Try also using a selection of different containers.

Tape recorded sounds. Record a selection of familiar sounds and voices and see if child can recognize them.

Singing and dancing

Children's first experience of making music usually comes when they join in songs or tunes with actions such as clapping, stamping, marching and jumping or by saying odd words they can remember. At first it comes as naturally to them to respond with movement as with sound, but they may become more inhibited about moving to music a little later on.

They learn to join in songs by hearing them constantly repeated. At first they often come in on the last word of a line and this gradually gives them the confidence to do more and more. Strong rhythm and rhyme help them to join in.

If a song has actions to go with it, remember that it is hard for small children to do the actions as well as singing, unless they know the song very well.

Action songs

If you're happy and you know it,
Clap your hands. (Clap, clap)
If you're happy and you know it,
Clap your hands. (Clap, clap)
If you're happy and you know it,
And you really want to show it,
If you're happy and you know it,
Clap your hands. (Clap, clap)

Other verses:
Shake your head
Touch your nose
Jump up and down
Stamp your feet

The wheels on the bus go round and round,
Round and round, round and round, (Move hands round
The wheels on the bus go round and round, in a circle.)
All day long.

Other verses:

The wipers on the bus go swish, swish, swish (Move forearms
from side to side.)

The people on the bus go up and down (Stand up, sit down.)
The horn on the bus goes peep, peep, peep (Press horn while
peeping.)

Oh, the Grand Old Duke of York, (March on the spot.)
He had ten thousand men,
He marched them up to the top of the hill, (March forwards.)
And he marched them down again. (March backwards.)

And when they were up they were up, (March forwards.)
And when they were down they were down, (March backwards.)
And when they were only half way up, (One step forwards and
They were neither up nor down. one step backwards.)

Below and on the next page are some popular action songs in case you cannot remember any. Don't worry if you do not know the tunes. Just choose any tune that seems to work, or make one up as you go along.

Wind the bobbin up, (Roll fists round in a
Wind the bobbin up, circle over each other.)
Pull, pull, (Pull fists outwards)
Clap, clap, clap. (Follow actions.)
Point to the ceiling,
Point to the floor,
Point to the window,
Point to the door.
Clap your hands together,
One, two three,
Put your hands upon your knee.

23

Head and shoulders, knees and toes,
Knees and toes.
Head and shoulders, knees and toes,
Knees and toes.
And eyes and ears and mouth and nose,
Head and shoulders, knees and toes,
Knees and toes.

Other verses: Touch head and shoulders but leave out the words for them. In the next verse leave out the words "Knees and toes". In the next one "eyes and ears" and finally "mouth and nose". After this silent verse sing the whole thing through loudly.

(Touch each part of the body as it is mentioned.)

Here we go round the mulberry bush,
The mulberry bush, the mulberry bush,
Here we go round the mulberry bush,
On a cold and frosty morning.

This is the way we wash our hands,
Wash our hands, wash our hands.
This is the way we wash our hands,
On a cold and frosty morning.

Other verses: This is the way we brush our hair, clean our teeth, wave goodbye.

(Skip round in a circle.)

(Do washing hands actions.)

Oh, we can play on the big brass drum,
And this is the music to it:
Boom, boom, boom goes the big brass drum,
And that's the way we do it.

Other verses: tambourine (jingle, jingle, jangle), castanets (click, click, clack)

Drumming action

Making up songs together

Start by playing around with a word that you know your child likes. Say it in lots of different ways – fast, slow, high, low. Develop a rhythm with it and then say something about it.

Caterpillar, caterpillar

You move very slowly.

Caterpillar, caterpillar

You're never in a hurry.

Build up a song by using lots of repetition with the occasional new statement. Don't worry about making rhymes unless they come very easily to you.

Say the words over and over again and then try singing them. It doesn't matter what it sounds like. Your child will still enjoy it even if you think you cannot sing a note.

When children first start to sing, they sing all on one note. Then they learn that their voices will go high and low and start to control them.

Some ideas for instruments to make

It is usually best to stick to percussion instruments with children under five. If you start by improvising them or making them at home, you will find out what goes down well. When you feel you have exhausted home-made possibilities you can find a wide range of very good children's percussion instruments in good toyshops.

Shakers

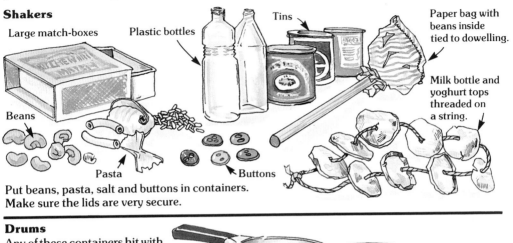

Large match-boxes   Plastic bottles   Tins   Paper bag with beans inside tied to dowelling.

Milk bottle and yoghurt tops threaded on a string.

Beans

Pasta   Buttons

Put beans, pasta, salt and buttons in containers. Make sure the lids are very secure.

Drums

Any of these containers hit with a wooden or metal spoon makes a good drum. You can also make drum heads by tying greaseproof paper over them.

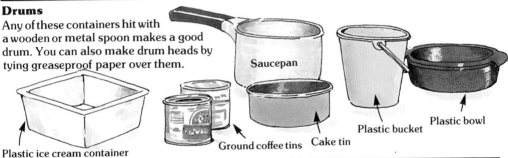

Saucepan

Plastic ice cream container

Ground coffee tins   Cake tin   Plastic bucket   Plastic bowl

Chimes

Hang metal objects on lengths of wool and hit with metal spoons.

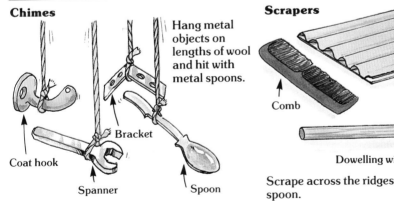

Coat hook

Bracket

Spanner   Spoon

Scrapers

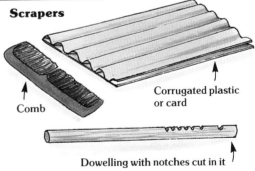

Comb   Corrugated plastic or card

Dowelling with notches cut in it

Scrape across the ridges with a pencil, ruler or spoon.

Learning to play an instrument

Most children do not start learning an instrument with a teacher until they are at least seven. A notable exception to this is the Suzuki method of learning the violin, piano or cello, in which children can start at about three. They do not learn from written music, but by imitation, through listening to records and playing games. Practice is done frequently but in small doses. The method undoubtedly works but requires the intimate involvement of a parent in every stage of the learning process.

PLAYING WITH WATER AND SAND

Children usually find playing with water or sand very soothing and relaxing. Remember, though, that small children can drown even in small amounts of water so never leave them playing with water on their own.

Water and sand play give children the opportunity to learn how natural materials behave and teach them about concepts such as quantity and capacity.

Physically, the play helps to develop their arm and hand muscles and improves their skill at pouring.

It is important to avoid the idea that getting wet or messy is naughty. Instead try to teach children to keep the mess within limits and make sure they help to clear up.

Baths and pools

Provide water and things to play with:

in the bath.

in a washing up bowl or baby bath.

at the sink.

on a tray.

Make sure children cannot burn themselves on water from a hot tap. Weather permitting, the ideal place for water play is outdoors but wherever they play, expect spills. If you want to prevent clothes getting wet, provide wellingtons and plastic macs or aprons. You can buy plastic cuffs to keep sleeves dry.

Things to play with in water

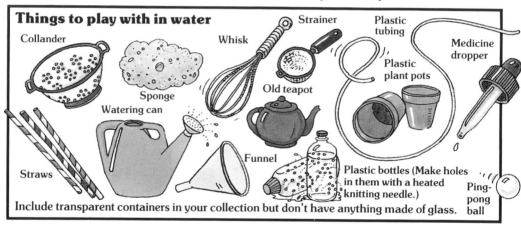

Collander

Sponge

Watering can

Straws

Whisk

Old teapot

Funnel

Strainer

Plastic tubing

Plastic plant pots

Medicine dropper

Plastic bottles (Make holes in them with a heated knitting needle.)

Ping-pong ball

Include transparent containers in your collection but don't have anything made of glass.

Sand and sandpits

You do not have to buy or make a sandpit. Fill an old tyre with sand or just use a small amount in an old washing up bowl or baby bath.

Buy silver sand rather than builder's sand which stains clothes and skin.

Cover sand kept outdoors to stop it getting waterlogged and dirty – cats love using sand pits as dirt trays.

You can clean sand by rinsing it with water containing baby bottle sterilizer.

Make a rule that sand must never be thrown. If sand gets in someone's eyes, rinse them with plenty of cold water.

Things to play with in sand

Dry sand behaves rather like water, so many of the containers for water play are suitable. You could also try:

Spoon

Scoop

Mould

Comb

Spade

Cup

Dustpan and brush

Games with water

Floating and Sinking. Encourage experiments with different objects. Do they float or sink? How fast do they sink?

Bottle tops (metal and plastic)
Spoons (metal and plastic)
Blocks of ice
Wooden bricks
Clothes-pegs
Polystyrene
Matches
Raisins
Marbles
Buttons
Corks
Twigs
Stones
Leaves

Boats. Half an orange peel
Paper cake cases
Polystyrene trays (from supermarket packets of fresh food)
Nut shells
Folded paper

Make masts from toothpicks or used matches and attach squares of paper for sails.

Bubbles. Show children how to make bubbles by blowing down straws or tubes into water, by trapping air bubbles under containers, or by squeezing empty detergent bottles.

Bubble recipe
1 part washing up liquid
2 parts water
To make bubbles stronger, add 1 tbspn glycerin per ½ litre (pint) of water.

Buy plastic blowers or use bent wire.

More things to try.

★ See what happens when salt, sugar, paper or glass is added to water.
★ Add food colouring to water. Children love pouring and mixing different colours.
★ Suggest bathing dolls, washing dolls' clothes and cleaning bikes and cars.
★ Provide a clean, empty paint tin filled with water and a large brush for "painting" the outside of the house.
★ Fill milk bottles with different amounts of water and tap them with a spoon to make different notes. This needs to be supervised so the bottles do not get broken.
★ Look at things underwater. Do hands look the same? What happens when you dip half a pencil into water?

Sand play ideas

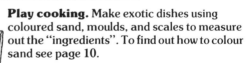

Miniature worlds.
Damp sand can be made into roads, bridges, tunnels, buildings. Add plastic or wooden vehicles, people or animals to make, say, a space station, town or farm.

Sand pictures. Use dry sand and a clean, flat surface. Pour the sand from a teapot or watering can so it makes a picture or pattern, or cover the surface with sand and let children draw in it with their fingers, a twig or a ruler.

Play cooking. Make exotic dishes using coloured sand, moulds, and scales to measure out the "ingredients". To find out how to colour sand see page 10.

Weighing and measuring. A set of scales, especially the balance type, provide a lot of fun in a sandpit. Provide paper bags and cartons so they can play "shop" and spoon goods for sale into them.

DRESSING UP AND PRETENDING

There are several reasons why children enjoy dressing up and pretending. Dressing up can be fun just for its own sake, for the feel of the various materials with their different texture, weight, warmth and colour.

In dressing up to become another person or creature, a child can begin to imagine how it feels to be someone else. In their fantasy play, children are able to control situations in which they would normally be powerless and this helps to build confidence. They are also able to act out their fears and worries and so start to come to terms with them.

Talking out loud during the play is an important stage in learning to think clearly. Eventually children become able to follow their own thoughts without actually giving voice to them. Fantasy play is equally common to both sexes. Parents sometimes worry if their sons dress up as fairies and princesses but this is quite normal.

On the practical side, dressing-up clothes should be simple to put on, should not be too long and have no dangerous cord round the neck. Children often regard dressing-up accessories, such as hats and bags, as more important than clothes.

Ideas for hats

Adapt hats by decorating them with things like ribbon, tissue paper, milk bottle tops, feathers and badges.

Try making simple hats out of card or thick paper. A basic cone shape is very adaptable.

Bands of different depths make different styles of hat.

Scarves or tea towels can make many different styles.

Things to collect

You can build up a good collection of dressing-up equipment from throw-outs. Ask friends and relatives, and look at jumble sales and in second-hand shops. Look for:

★ hats, bags, belts, gloves;
★ old jewellery, slides, bows, ribbons, spectacle frames, sunglasses;
★ scarves, stoles, shawls, aprons, petticoats, nightdresses;

★ lengths of material, such as curtains, tablecloths, sheets, bedspreads, towels. These are useful for making cloaks, saris, and togas, and also playhouses and tents;
★ shoes. It is best to choose shoes which will fit over your child's own shoes. High heels are not very safe for under-fives.

Store everything together in, say, a large box or laundry basket but keep small items such as jewellery in a separate container. A mirror, preferably a full-length one, is fairly essential for dressing-up sessions.

Making jewellery

Pasta jewellery. Paint pieces of macaroni and other types of pasta which have a hole in them. When they are dry, thread them on shirring elastic to make necklaces, bracelets and ear-rings.

Card and paper jewellery. Make ear-rings, medallions, brooches and hair decorations like the ones shown below.

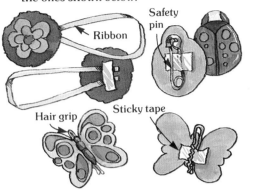

Safety pin

Ribbon

Hair grip

Sticky tape

Playdough jewellery. Make pendants, brooches and ear-rings out of playdough baked in the oven. (See page 13 for the recipe.) When cool, paint with poster paints and, if you want a more professional finish, varnish.

Tape a safety pin to the back of brooches, as shown above.

Bits and pieces

- ★ False teeth (made from orange peel)
- ★ Spectacles (made from pipe cleaners)
- ★ Binoculars (toilet rolls)
- ★ Telescope (kitchen roll)
- ★ Various types of boots (decorated wellingtons)
- ★ Broken leg (wellington with strips of old sheet wrapped round it)
- ★ Soldier's hat (colander)
- ★ Chain mail (painted string vest)
- ★ Nurse's hat (shirt collar, starched if possible)

Making masks

Make a basic mask shape out of cardboard, for example a cereal packet or a paper plate. Cut two eye holes and a flap for the nose, and make a hole at either side.

Put rubber bands through the holes so they will fit over the ears, or just use ribbon, elastic or pipe cleaners to hold the mask on.

If your child dislikes the mask pressing against his face, try putting it on a stick instead.

Decorate with crayons or paints. You can also glue on hair (see below) and use glitter, sequins, gummed stars, bottle tops (for noses), split peas (for warts) and sticking plaster (for wounds).

For animal masks, stick on felt or fabric to represent fur and cut ears out of cardboard or stiff paper. Pipe cleaners make good whiskers; straws with cardboard circles on top good antennae.

Hair

Wool, cotton wool, raffia, string and wood-shavings all make good hair. Glue them to a mask or inside the rim of a hat. For curly hair, use wool unravelled from an old jumper or curl thin strips of paper round a pencil.

Wool glued to hat.

Curls on mask.

Old tights or stockings.

For beards and moustaches, glue the pretend hair to a cardboard or fabric base. Make holes in either side and fasten around the head in the same way as a mask.

Face paint

Discarded make-up or a packet of face paints provides a lot of entertainment. To clean them off afterwards, use cold cream and cotton wool followed by soap and water.

29

Play kits

Here are some ideas for pretend play situations.

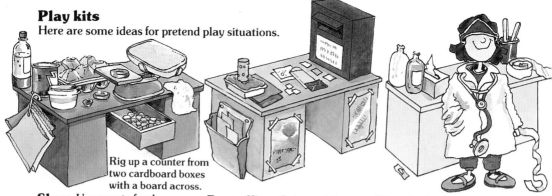

Rig up a counter from two cardboard boxes with a board across.

Shop. Use empty food packets and unopened tins, put the prices on sticky labels, have a toy cash register or use a shoe box as a till. Make money from milk bottle tops, cardboard and paper.

Post office. Cut up sticky labels for stamps. Save old stamp books, postcards and envelopes. Cut a slit in a box for posting. Have a stamp pad (kitchen paper soaked in paint) and a stamp (a cork).

Hospital. Use strips of material for bandages and masking tape for plasters. Save small plastic bottles. A small syringe (without the needle) and a toy stethoscope are both fairly cheap to buy.

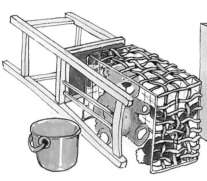

Zoo. Turn chairs with bars on to their sides and use fireguards to make cages. Put toy animals inside and provide a bucket so the keeper can feed them.

Aeroplane cockpit. Paint a large cardboard box or cover with coloured paper, then stick on a mass of knobs and dials made from bottle tops, jars and tubes.

Car. Add paper plate wheels and steering wheel to a big cardboard box. Paint a number plate on card. Use a sardine can key or any unused keys. Coloured tape makes good trim.

Playhouses and dens

There are many ways of making children their own private places to play in. Old curtains, sheets and blankets are useful, and so are giant cardboard boxes of the type new fridges and cookers are packed in. Whether the den represents a house, spaceship or cave, you will probably be asked to supply cooking and cleaning equipment, tables, seats and beds.

Table

Clothes-horse

Outdoor washing line

Cardboard box

Ring of chairs

Miniature worlds

Cardboard boxes of assorted shapes and sizes can represent almost any type of building, such as a house, garage, farm or castle. Shoe boxes are especially useful. Pipe cleaners, plasticine and playdough are good for making people, animals, furniture and vehicles.

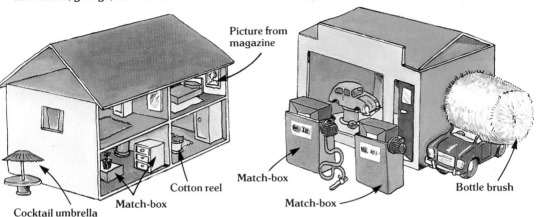

Picture from magazine

Cotton reel

Match-box

Match-box

Match-box

Bottle brush

Cocktail umbrella

You can make a simple background for miniature buildings, people and objects by joining large sheets of paper together and drawing in roads, rivers, railways and fields with felt pen.

<hr>

Puppets

Puppets are probably the easiest kind of "person" toy to make. Using them often encourages children to express hidden thoughts or feelings and to look at situations from a different viewpoint. (Specialists often use puppets with shy children and children with speech and other communication problems.)

Some children just play with puppets in the same way as they do with dolls. Some may want to put on a show. Some children dislike puppets and puppet shows so don't force them if they are not interested.

Paper bags. Draw a face on a bag, twist the corners for ears and hold in place on the child's hand with a rubber band round the wrist.

Socks. Stick or sew eyes on to an old sock. Show children how to put their hands inside and pull the toe of the sock in between their fingers and thumb to make a mouth.

Wooden spoons. Draw a face on a spoon and drape a scrap of material around the handle for a cloak.

Paper or felt. Make finger puppets by cutting out semi-circles, curling them into a tube shape and sticking them, so that they just fit over the fingers. Draw or stick on eyes, noses, ears and hats.

Match-boxes. Take the outside part of a match-box and glue on paper shapes for noses, eyes and ears. Use as a finger puppet.

Card. Cut an animal shape out of card. Cut two holes at the bottom to allow the fingers to poke through and act as legs.

31

IN THE KITCHEN

Children can get great satisfaction from making things and then eating them, and the kitchen provides them with endless opportunities for learning.

It gives them their first taste of science and the chance to learn about concepts such as quantity, shape and time. It can improve their counting and reading, increase their vocabulary, develop their manipulative skills and teach them how to concentrate and cooperate with another person.

An added bonus for parents is that cooking can sometimes help to cure fussy eaters.

Children need constant supervision when they are cooking and take a long time to do things, so if you are in a hurry don't let them join in.

There are several things in the kitchen that children might enjoy sorting into groups. Try giving them the cutlery tray, various root vegetables, different types of pasta or beans, or tins. If your scales are the balance type, you could give them an assortment of objects to balance and weigh. Or, if you can spare some cheap ingredients such as flour, oats, rice or pasta, let them do some play cooking with these. They can also learn a lot just by watching you cook.

Cooking tips and hints

Mixing or mashing. Put a damp cloth under the bowl or pan to stop it slipping.

Rolling out pastry. Explain how to dust the rolling pin and board with flour to stop the pastry sticking. A flour shaker is useful for this.

Greasing baking tins. Explain how to tilt the tin to catch the light so she can see if it has been greased thoroughly.

Sieving. Explain how to tap the side of the sieve rather than shaking it about. This stops the contents flying everywhere.

Decorating. Adding the final touches to a dish makes children feel they have had a big hand in making it even if they have done none of the preparation.

Cutting. Start with a blunt knife and soft foods like bananas or bread, then cheese, before moving on to slightly sharper knives and harder fruits and vegetables.

Measuring ingredients. Start by measuring in cupfuls and spoonfuls. Balance scales are much easier for children to understand than spring scales and make good playthings.

Following recipes. If your child is starting to recognize letters and numbers, you can write out your own simplified version of favourite recipes for him to follow.

Safety and rules

Young children should always be supervised by an adult when they are cooking. For safety's sake it is worth making a few rules to follow in the kitchen.

★ Get together everything you will need before you start so that you do not have to leave your child unsupervised.

★ Teach children to wash their hands before cooking.

★ Teach them to be very careful when handling knives.

★ Teach them to ask before tasting anything.

★ If you spill something, clear it up immediately. One of you might slip on it.

★ If you use an electric mixer, teach children to keep their hands behind their back while it is on. Never put anything into the bowl while the mixer is going round.

★ Only do cook-in-the-oven recipes and don't let your child use the grill or rings. Turn saucepan handles so that they do not stick out over the edge of the cooker.

Making biscuits

Biscuits give plenty of scope for measuring, mixing, rolling out, shape-cutting and decorating. Below is a good basic biscuit recipe. Younger children will probably enjoy decorating them most.

Basic biscuit recipe

125g (4oz) soft margarine
 or butter
125g (4oz) sugar
 (white or brown)
250g (8oz) plain flour
1 egg
Pinch of salt

Beat the margarine and sugar together then beat the egg and add it to the mixture. Sift in the flour and salt, and mix to form a ball of dough. Roll out the dough and cut it into shapes. Put on a greased tray and bake in a moderate oven (approximately 190°C or gas mark 5) for about 15 minutes.

Decoration. Make a simple glacé icing from icing sugar and hot water (about 100g (3½oz) icing sugar to 1 tablespoon water) and perhaps a few drops of food colouring. Spread the icing on the biscuits with a knife or use a plastic icing syringe to make patterns, pictures or letters.

Decorate the biscuits with an assortment of the following: bought cake decorations, small sweets, dried fruit, chopped nuts, chopped glacé cherries and desiccated coconut. To avoid too much mess, put out the decorations in an empty egg box.

Experimenting with flavour. For biscuits with different flavours, try adding to the basic mixture some grated lemon or orange rind, melted or grated chocolate, mixed spice, cinnamon, ginger, dried fruit, chopped nuts, mixed peel or glacé cherries.

To make savoury biscuits, leave out the sugar and add some grated cheese or yeast spread. For sandwich biscuits, use a filling of jam, or icing sugar and butter creamed together.

Other things to try

Bread. Kneading is the part children enjoy. Lightly oil children's hands to stop the dough sticking to them. Divide the dough into small, manageable pieces.

Scones. Suggest making them into animal shapes or people and give them currant eyes.

Jam tarts. If you don't want to make pastry, buy some ready-made. Children enjoy rolling it out, cutting it into circles and putting them into a greased bun tin. Fill with jam, or mix golden syrup and breadcrumbs together to make treacle tarts.

Uncooked sweets. You can make peppermint creams, sugar mice or coconut creams from fondant icing (approximately 500g (1lb) of icing sugar to 1 egg white). Add a few drops of food colouring or flavouring as you choose.

Cake. Choose a basic all-in-one recipe. Children like tiny individual cakes in *petit-fours* cases. Decorate as for biscuits.

Drinks. If you have a blender you could try letting children make milk shakes, yoghurt drinks and fruit drinks.

Brandysnaps. The fun lies in trying to roll them round the handle of a spoon to make hollow pipes.

GROWING THINGS

Growing things makes children begin to realize where living things come from and what they need to survive. It also helps them to develop a sense of responsibility as they learn that plants will die if they do not look after them properly. It teaches them the difference between things grown just to look at and things grown to eat, and gives them an idea of the origins of various products.

Concentrate on quick-growing plants so your child does not lose interest before anything has happened and remember that home-grown plants make good presents.

Cress

Cress is a favourite for children because it grows very quickly on almost any damp surface and you can eat it in sandwiches and salads.

Try growing it on cotton wool, several layers of kitchen roll or an old flannel or sponge.

Wet the growing surface, then pour off any excess water and sprinkle cress seeds thinly over it. Keep it warm and damp and within two or three days the cress should start to grow.

You can grow mustard mixed with cress but it tastes a bit strong for most children.

You can also grow grass seed, bird seed and even guinea-pig food in the same way. Make sure your child does not eat the results.

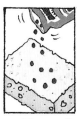

Cress words. Write your initials in seeds and watch them grow.

Cress clown. Draw a clown's face on an empty egg shell with felt pen. Fill the shell with damp cotton wool or kitchen roll and sprinkle cress seeds on top. Wait for the clown's hair to grow.

Miniature gardens

Provide an old meat tin or foil dish and collect damp earth, sand, moss, pebbles, twigs and flowers to arrange into a temporary garden. You could try growing some real grass seed. Include an old mirror for a pond or put water in a small, flat container and camouflage it. Add toy animals and people to the garden.

Other things to try

Broad beans or peas. Soak the beans or peas in water for 24 hours. Line a jam jar with damp kitchen roll and put about 2½cm (1in) of water in the bottom. Put the beans or peas between the paper and the glass, about half way down the jar. Put the jar in a light place and watch the roots and shoots forming.

Fruit pips. Soak orange, lemon or grapefruit pips in water for a day. Put them in a pot of soil or potting compost and cover them with ½cm (¼in) of the soil. Moisten. Put the pot in a polythene bag and loosely tie the top. Put in a warm place and keep the soil moist. Shoots should appear within a few days.

You can also grow peach, cherry or plum stones like this. Before potting, crack the stone without damaging the kernel.

LEARNING ABOUT ANIMALS

Children are naturally fascinated by animals and need to be given the opportunity to learn about them, perhaps through trips to places like zoos and farm parks. They can learn not to be afraid of animals but to have respect for them and, by extension, for all forms of life. Learning about animals also provides a good introduction to the subjects of birth, death and reproduction.

First pets

Though children can learn a lot from being pet owners, they cannot fulfil the responsibilities involved without a great deal of help. It may be better just to borrow small creatures from the wild for a short time. You can observe and care for them together, then let them go free.

Containers. Always provide as large a container as possible. Glass makes it easiest for you to observe the creatures. A small fish tank is ideal but a large pyrex dish or a glass bowl or jar will do. If a cover is necessary, punch air holes in it or use muslin.

Caterpillars. Look for these in hedgerows and gardens. Remove them gently with a paintbrush and take some of the plant you find them on. Don't keep more than three or four together and don't mix types. First they turn into chrysalises, then, after two or three weeks, into moths or butterflies. If they do not emerge after that time, spray them with a little water. Let the moths and butterflies go free.

Worms. Put alternate layers of sand and soil in your container. Then put in a few worms from the garden and some leaves for them to feed on. Keep the soil damp. Watch the worms working their way down through the layers and leaving their casts on the surface.

Other creatures. You could also try keeping snails, earwigs, woodlice or ladybirds. Always take some of the plant you find them on and put them in damp soil. Let them go free after a few days.

Feeding wild birds and animals

Birds. When you start feeding birds, they come to rely on you so continue feeding them right through the winter. Put the food high up out of the way of cats, somewhere where you will have a good view from a window. Different birds like:

Seeds (Collect from plants or buy bird seed.)
Bread
Bacon rind
Cheese
Dried fruit
Banana
Coconut
Peanuts (with or without shells but not salted)
Peanut butter
Suet

Make a bird pudding by mixing up scraps of these foods with melted fat and letting it set. Birds also need water to drink and bathe in.

Hedgehogs. You may be able to attract a hedgehog to your garden by leaving out some dog food or a saucer of water.

Squirrels. Feed them on seeds and nuts. Take some with you if you are going for a walk amongst trees.

Thinking of buying a pet

Make sure you know exactly what is involved in the care and feeding of any animal, bird or fish you are thinking of keeping as a pet. Don't buy anything without considering all the disadvantages very carefully. It can be a good idea to start with something very simple like a goldfish.

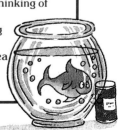

COLLECTING THINGS

Children can learn a lot from making collections. An early enthusiasm for something could lead on to an interesting hobby later, and deciding how to keep, arrange or display things can provide useful opportunities for sorting and classifying. Many commercial toy companies trade shamelessly on the collector's instinct in children. Having their own special collections might make them slightly less susceptible to the pressures of the advertisers.

You may have to help by generating ideas, but don't pressurize a child to make a collection – some simply don't have the collector's instinct. Here are some things a child might get pleasure from collecting.

Tickets, e.g. bus and train tickets, tickets to the zoo, the cinema and other entertainments. Stick in scrapbooks with descriptions or drawings of outings.

Pebbles. Collect pretty shapes or colours. Also, encourage children to collect big, smooth pebbles and paint them or write and draw on them with felt pens.

Postcards. Collect as souvenirs and encourage friends and relations to send them whenever they are away from home.

Sweet wrappers, stamps, stickers. Use them to make colourful posters.

Badges. These often come free for promotional purposes or with donations to charity. Collect or make them (see page 44) and display on board covered with felt.

Feathers. Having something to collect on walks makes them more interesting. This could well lead on to a real interest in birds.

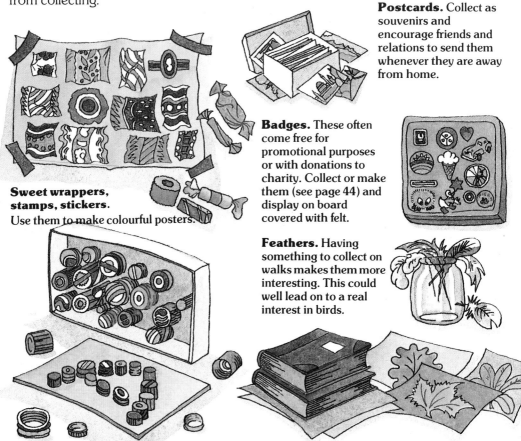

Bottle tops. Collect the tops of all sorts of different kinds of screw-top bottles, jars and tibes. Arrange in patterns or letter shapes.

Leaves. These are easier for small children to collect than flowers. Show them how to preserve leaves by pressing them between blotting paper under a pile of books.

GETTING EXERCISE

Exercise benefits almost everyone. It improves mood, appetite and quality of sleep and brings better general health. It is specially important for children – it develops their muscles, increases their strength and agility, and improves their coordination, balance and sense of timing. It also increases their understanding of the concepts of distance, height and space. Many children learn a lot about how to socialize with other children by joining in physical activities.

The amount and type of exercise children get obviously depends on individual circumstances: whether you have a garden or use parks and playgrounds, whether you have access to gym or movement and dance classes. It also depends on a child's inclinations; some children are naturally much more physically active than others.

Most children rarely attempt anything beyond their capabilities. It is best to interfere as little as possible when they are attempting some physical feat or you may actually increase the likelihood of an accident. Watch out, though, when they are playing with older children or are being goaded beyond their abilities.

Outdoor obstacle course

Below are some ideas to help you set up an obstacle course in the garden. You could also use some of them to help you set up an obstacle course for a tricycle, scooter or bicycle.

Old bucket with hole in the bottom

Netting (could use old sheet or groundsheet)

Paving stone (stepping stone)

Flower pot (stepping stone)

Old pillow case stuffed with newspaper

Cardboard boxes (tunnel)

Plank (ramp)

Old tyre

Log for balancing on

GOING SWIMMING

There are many good reasons for taking children swimming as early as possible: the younger they are the easier it is to learn to swim; children with some experience of swimming are safer when playing in or near water; swimming is excellent all-round exercise; it helps to develop breathing control and can be very relaxing; it is something the whole family can enjoy together and is often a good way to meet other children and parents.

Small children generally get on best if they are introduced to the water by one of their parents. If you yourself feel nervous of the water, try to go with another adult who is confident. Go to a shallow children's pool and if possible enrol in parent and child swimming classes.

Your general aim should be to get your child to enjoy himself in the water and to move freely backwards, forwards and sideways on his front and on his back, probably with buoyancy aids.

Keep each session short. Your child will learn more in short frequent visits than the occasional long one. Always get out before he begins to get cold, as small children's temperature regulating system is not yet very efficient.

Developing water confidence

The first step towards enjoying swimming is feeling confident in the water. You can do quite a lot at home to build a child's water confidence. Encourage him to get his face and head wet and to blow bubbles in the bath. Provide as many opportunities as possible for playing with water (see pages 26 and 27).

On your first visit to a swimming pool with your child it is a good idea to have a look around without actually swimming. This will give him a chance to see what will happen and get used to the strange atmosphere, noise and smell. Look at the changing rooms and lockers and talk about what you will do when you come next time. This will make you feel more confident as well, which in turn will affect your child's attitude.

Swimming pool facilities

Swimming pool facilities vary considerably. It may be worth your while to travel a little further than you need to find one with really good facilities for small children. Things to find out:

★ What is the normal temperature of the water? Small children will be put off if the water is too cold. It needs to be at least 27°C (80°F).

★ Is there a separate pool for small children? It is very helpful to be away from the rough and tumble of the main pool.

★ Taking toys such as boats, beach balls, watering cans and bath toys will help to make a child feel at home in the water.

★ How do you get into the pool? Some children are happier if they can walk into the water instead of being carried. Wide, shallow steps or a gentle slope are best. If you have to climb down a ladder, let someone else hold your child, or sit him on the edge while you get in.

★ How deep is the shallow water? It is an advantage if there is an area of very shallow water where a child can sit, crawl or splash about.

★ Is the floor in the changing rooms and around the pool non-slip?

★ Are there classes for parents and children? These are a very good idea, especially if you yourself do not feel confident in the water.

Things to do in the water

Hold your child close and bounce gently up and down in the water, so that you both get your shoulders wet.

Legs apart, one foot slightly in front of the other gives best balance.

Hold your child away from you and bounce up and down, then move forwards and backwards through the water.

Keep face on level with child's to give her confidence

Hold him under his chest and hips and encourage leg kicking and arm movement.

If child seems confident enough, let go.

Once he is used to the water on his body, get him used to splashes on his face and head.

Encourage him to put his face in the water and to blow bubbles.

Encourage her to put her head under the water and to open her eyes

Get her to move through the water by kicking and paddling. She may be fairly upright at first.

Encourage him to adopt a more horizontal position and then to push off from the side and glide.

When she is confident, encourage jumping in from the side.

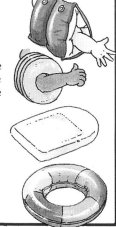

Armbands and floats

Arm bands are really the best floating aid. They should be worn above the elbows. The double-chambered kind are the safest. You can gradually reduce the amount of air in them until they are no longer needed. Many children refuse to wear them at first, but if allowed just to play with them they usually consent in the end.

Polystyrene floats are useful for encouraging horizontal movement.

Rings tend to restrict movement and small children can fall out of them.

Water safety

Small children should always be closely supervised by an adult when near water, even if they can swim quite well. If they fall into cold water they can get into trouble very quickly.

You should always accompany them into the sea and insist that they stay in shallow water. Don't let them play on inflatable rafts or air beds and take any warning notices very seriously.

OUTINGS AND JOURNEYS

Children need to get out and about and benefit from experiencing as many different situations as possible. Remember that any walk or outing becomes more fun if it has a specific goal.

Children will feel more involved in an outing if you plan it with them beforehand and talk about it together afterwards. Use books and make pictures to follow up some of the things you have seen together.

Ideas for outings

The kind of outings you go on will obviously depend on your individual circumstances. The local paper and local library are good places to look for information about any special events in your area. Here are a few simple, general ideas for things to do.

Try a different form of transport from your usual one: for example, a short bus ride if you usually travel by car.

Go for a short train ride from your nearest station and back again.

Watch trains, especially at bridges or tunnels.

Watch boats on rivers or canals.

Watch aeroplanes. Most airports have a viewing platform.

Watch a building site, or roadworks.

Watch cars at a car wash.

Go on a picnic. You do not have to go far or take much with you.

Send yourselves a letter. Post it from your local box at collection time.

Get high up in, say, a department store or block of flats and spot landmarks.

Going shopping

Children enjoy shopping most if you let them get really involved. Let them look in the cupboards to see what is needed and help you make the shopping list. At the shops, they can find the goods on the shelves and hand the money to the cashier. When you can, make use of the things that specially appeal to children such as lifts, escalators and self-opening doors.

Shopping cards. Use pieces of card about the size of a postcard. On each card draw or stick a picture of something you frequently need to include on your shopping list. You could use distinctive bits of packaging on some of the cards. When you go shopping children can take the appropriate cards and help you find what you want by matching them to the goods on the shelves.

Games to play on journeys

Guessing games

★ How long is a minute starting from now?

★ How fast are we going?

★ Are we going to turn right or left next?

★ What colour will the next traffic light be at?

★ How long does it take to go a mile starting from now?

★ Who or what am I? Give clues, for example, "I am soft and furry and I purr"; "you use me to heat water".

Spotting games

★ I-Spy. Use colours instead of letters.

★ Choose a colour. The first to spot a car that colour chooses the next colour.

★ What will be the next animal we see?

★ Shout "rat-tat" if you see a post-box and "ring-ring" if you see a telephone box. First to spot either wins.

★ Cross your fingers if you see an ambulance or fire engine. Don't uncross them until you see a policeman or police car.

Other games

★ Keep quiet, or talk or sing for a minute.

★ One person asks questions. The others take it in turns to answer but must not say "yes", "no", "black" or "white".

★ One person says a word, for example "party". The next says a word she associates with the first, for example "jelly". And so on.

★ One person starts telling a story. The others take it in turns to add a section to it.

★ What's your name? Choose a letter of the alphabet and take it in turns to give a name starting with that letter. When you get stuck, you are out.

Ideas for long journeys

These take a little time to prepare.

Vehicle pictures. Cut out pictures of vehicles from magazines and put them in a large envelope or bag. Children take out one at a time and have to spot a vehicle to match it before moving on to the next one.

Lucky dip. Make a bag of surprises by wrapping up tiny presents individually. Ration them to last through the journey. Here are a few ideas for things to wrap:

Food: a few raisins, sweets or biscuits.

Toys: small pencils and notepads, a magic slate, puzzles and tricks, colouring pads.

For those who can read or recognize some letters: a secret message, name of a game to play, a song to sing.

Journey tapes. Make a tape and include stories, or one story in instalments, jokes, riddles, poems, songs and suggestions for games and things to spot.

PARTIES

It is not really practical to give children a proper party before they are three. Until then, it is better just to have a few friends to tea.

The key to a successful party is to plan ahead very carefully. This is vital. Keep the numbers small and the length of the party short. Two hours is long enough for three-year-olds. Put the starting and finishing time on the invitations.

Prepare more games than you think you will need. Keep each one short and stick to games with very simple rules that the children are likely to know already. Alternate energetic and quieter games and have a quiet one after tea and before the children go home.

Under-sevens cannot cope with too much competition, so adapt games to make them non-competitive or fix them so that everyone has a chance to win. If you have prizes, make sure that everyone wins one.

Other tips on avoiding disasters

★ Enlist other adults as helpers.

★ Make sure you have all the parents' telephone numbers.

★ Hide away any toys your child does not want to share.

★ Organize visits to the toilet for everyone after tea.

★ Plan the party with your child so that he knows what is going to happen and does not have unrealistic expectations.

When the music stops

When you are playing musical games, try to make sure that the players cannot see exactly when the music is going to be turned on and off.

Musical bumps. Everyone jumps up and down in time to the music. Each time it stops, they all sit down. Pick out the last one to sit down, but don't make them sit out for the rest of the game. The winners can be the ones who have never been last.

Musical balloons. Have one fewer balloon than there are players. When the music stops each player has to grab a balloon. Spot the person without a balloon.

Hot potato. Everyone sits in a circle and passes round a potato. When the music stops, whoever has the potato must do a forfeit, such as run round the circle and sit down again.

Pass the parcel. Everyone sits in a circle and passes round a parcel with several layers of wrapping on it. When the music stops, the person holding the parcel starts unwrapping it. To sustain interest, try putting a little present between each layer of wrapping and fix the music stops so everyone gets a chance to do some unwrapping and find a present.

Songs and stories

Action rhymes and songs go down well, if you have someone who is prepared to lead the singing. See page 23 to remind you of specific songs.

Similarly, you could have a story after tea if someone is willing to read or tell one.

Games for a limited space

Simon says. One person is Simon. He stands facing the others and shouts out instructions, such as "Simon says, 'touch your toes' ". Everyone has to obey. But if he leaves out the "Simon says", anyone who obeys the instruction is "out". As for musical bumps, it is best not to make the person sit out while you carry on until there is an overall winner.

Children find it quite hard to catch each other out, so limit the time everyone has as Simon and let adults have turns as well.

Duck, duck, goose. Everyone sits in a circle and one player is It. He walks round the outside of the circle, tapping each person lightly on the head and saying "Duck" with each tap. Finally, he taps and says "Goose". The goose jumps up and chases It round the outside of the circle. If It gets back to the empty space before Goose catches him, Goose becomes It.

Hunt the thimble/slipper/teddy/sweets. You can either have one thing to hunt, which gets hidden again each time someone finds it, or have the same number of things hidden as there are children at the party. Hunting for little presents or sweets to take home makes a good ending to a party. You will have to stop some children from finding more than their fair share.

Squeak, piggy, squeak. Everyone sits on the floor except for one player, who is blindfolded. He tries to catch hold of the others. Each time he does, he says "Squeak, piggy, squeak" and the person has to squeak. If he guesses who it is, the squeaker is blindfolded.

Sneaky Peter. One person is blindfolded and sits on a chair with a teddy underneath it. The others try to sneak the teddy away without him catching hold of them. When someone is caught, he becomes It.

Sideshow activities

If you have a large party room and an extra adult to supervise, you can have these going on as the guests arrive or during the party for people who do not want to join in the main game.

Guessing games
★ How many sweets in the saucer?
★ How long is a minute?
★ What can you feel in the bag?
★ What food is it? (Blindfold tasting)

Throwing games
★ Throw the beanbag in the basket.
★ Throw the ping-pong balls in the jar.
★ Drop the clothes-pegs in the bottle.

Party themes

You could give a party with a special theme, which you can carry through the invitations, decorations and cake. Choose the theme with your child. You can rename all the games to fit the theme.

If you want the children to wear fancy dress, choose a theme for which outfits can be created quite simply – perhaps have a hat party or party with a colour theme.

Special entertainments

If you decide to lay on a special entertainment, such as a puppet show or conjuring act, make it no longer than half an hour. Check that you will not get a repeat of a show done recently in your area and make contingency plans in case the entertainer does not turn up or is late.

43

Wet afternoons and other difficult times

Many of the other chapters in this book will give you ideas for the times when you cannot take children out and they are feeling fed up and need to get involved in some absorbing activity.

You may like to keep a box of toys for use only on these occasions, or have a secret selection of colouring books and puzzle books tucked away. Story tapes can also come in handy, especially for children who are not feeling well. The selection of ideas on these two pages may also be useful.

Catching cone

Make a cone and attach a ping-pong ball, or some other light object to it. Try to catch the ball in the cone.

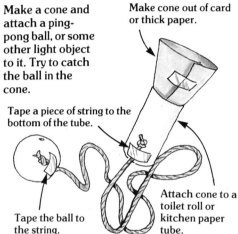

Make cone out of card or thick paper.

Tape a piece of string to the bottom of the tube.

Tape the ball to the string.

Attach cone to a toilet roll or kitchen paper tube.

Sewing cards

Use old Christmas or birthday cards, or draw very simple pictures on pieces of card. Make holes along the outline of the objects in the pictures. Thread a large, blunt needle with wool or embroidery silk, so that your child can sew round the outlines. Instead of needle and thread you could use long shoelaces or string, stiffened at the end with sellotape.

Skittles

Use empty plastic bottles as your skittles and a fairly large ball. Start by standing quite close. A narrow hallway is an ideal place to play. If you do not have any plastic bottles you could use yoghurt pots or plastic cups stuffed with newspaper. Instead of a ball, try rolling a potato.

Fun with balloons

Blow up balloons, then let them go to see whose goes the furthest. Use felt pens to make them look like insects, monsters or members of the family.

Attach a piece of string between two chairs and use bats or hands to have a game of balloon tennis.

Badges

Help children to cut out badge shapes from pieces of card. Squares, oblongs and triangles are easier to cut than circles. Decorate with felt pens and coloured sticky paper. Attach safety pins to the back with sticky tape or sticking plaster.

Torch tag

Each person has a torch and directs its beam on to the ceiling in a darkened room. One of the spots of light is "It" and has to try and catch the others. If you have any tissue paper or coloured cellophane, you could put a different colour over each torch, using rubber bands to hold them in place. When one light catches another the colours mix.

Magnets

It is worth buying a large horseshoe magnet for children to experiment with. They can have a lot of fun just testing to see what is magnetic and what is not. If you have some paper clips, you could make paper characters to slot into them, as shown on the right. Put the characters on a piece of flat cardboard propped up on two piles of books, and use the magnet underneath the cardboard to move them around. You could make up a story and move each character as it is mentioned.

Paper darts

Follow the steps shown here to make paper darts. See who can throw their dart furthest or make one land on the table. It can take a bit of practice to learn how to throw a dart.

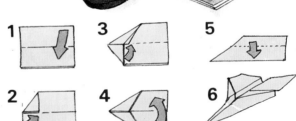

1

2

3

4

5

6

Stunts

Get children to try doing these things:

★ Rub stomach in a circle with one hand, while patting head with the other.

★ Make a "3" in the air with one hand, while making an "0" in the air with the other.

★ Stand facing someone and copy every movement that they make, as though they were a mirror.

★ Sing one nursery rhyme, such as "Baa, baa, black sheep", while someone else sings another one, such as "Ring a ring o'roses".

Wet afternoon box

Here is a selection of things you might find it useful to keep in a special box which you keep for use when you have run out of other ideas and the situation looks desperate:

Soft ball (felt or foam for use indoors)
Ping-pong balls
Torches and spare batteries
Horseshoe magnet
Balloons
Sticky paper shapes
Old Christmas and birthday cards
Magnifying glass (Look at all sorts of things – hands, pictures, writing, food, carpets, sponges.)

45

THE STUDY OF PLAY

A hundred years ago few people would have looked upon play as having an important part in a child's development. Playing was something children did when they had nothing more important to do. Today there is a growing interest in the relationship between play and human development. Many universities now have departments or units devoted to the study of this subject and most of the research is now concentrated on the pre-school years. The growth of pre-school play provision, and of play provision for older children, is a visible result of the growing interest in and belief in the importance of play.

The development of the study of play

Interest in play developed alongside the realisation that the conditions and experiences of childhood had an important effect upon later life. The work of philosophers, such as Rousseau, and naturalists, such as Darwin, challenged and eventually changed the view that children were little adults developing according to some preordained plan. This changed view of childhood naturally led on to an interest in play.

Early views of play saw it as a principally physical activity – a way of releasing surplus energy no longer required purely for survival. As the field of psychology developed, so did more sophisticated views of play and childhood. Play was seen to involve intellectual and emotional activity as well as physical.

Theories about play

Many different theories about play have been developed over the years, but the main areas of approach can be seen in the work of three great psychologists: Sigmund Freud, Jean Piaget and Jerome Bruner.

Freud was concerned with the function of play in emotional development. His work focussed on fantasy play and, in particular, on the link between play and a person's unconscious self. He claimed that the unconscious finds expression through play, and he developed two explanations for how this might operate. Firstly, children play in order to gain control of unpleasant feelings; and secondly children play to fulfill unconscious desires. Although much of Freud's work is now being questioned, it is still generally accepted that play is a way in which children can express their feelings and work through emotional disturbances.

Freud's approach contrasts strongly with that of the Swiss psychologist, Jean Piaget, whose theories of how the intellect develops underpin much modern educational practice. Piaget undertook many experiments to establish the link between play and intellectual development. Broadly speaking, he saw play as a means of practising what has been learnt, of perfecting newly acquired skills, and of demonstrating that new skills had been learnt and perfected.

Both Freud and Piaget believed that children outgrew play once their emotional and intellectual skills had reached a certain point of development and this aspect of their work is strongly contested today. Piaget's work is also criticised by more modern theorists for denying play a more active role in the way children learn. Bruner, for example, sees play as a means of actively acquiring information, constructing new ideas and developing skills.

Who studies play and why?

The bulk of investigation into play is still undertaken by psychologists interested in child development. They want to understand the role of play in development, which types of play effect which aspects of development, and what conditions are most effective for stimulating play.

This investigation is of interest to, and also undertaken by, a range of other specialists: educational psychologists are interested in the use of play as a method of learning; psychiatrists are interested in play as a form of therapy; sociologists are interested in play as a means of developing social skills and achieving social integration.

The other main area of interest is shown by naturalists and biologists interested in the role of play in the evolution of the species, and whether it is an integral part of the process of creating and adapting to change.

Types of play

For research purposes play tends to be divided up into categories. The number of subdivisions can be endless, but in general there are five main categories each of which benefits different aspects of development:

1. Physical play – develops coordination, strength, stamina, suppleness, spatial awareness, key controlling skills (e.g. catching and throwing) and positive physical self-image.
2. Discovery play – affects general intellectual development, the capacity to approach problems creatively and to solve them, the capability of moving through the various stages of conceptual development and the capacity for abstract thought later in life.
3. Social play – influences general social development, the ability to collaborate and cooperate with others, communication skills, sense of self in relation to others and ability to survive in groups.

4. Fantasy play – provides opportunities to express emotions, to act out and resolve or reconcile disturbing aspects of existence, to act out and achieve desires and ambitions beyond the scope of real life and to develop an imaginative capacity.
5. Creative play – develops small-scale coordination skill, conceptual, abstract and lateral thinking skills, creative responses to problems and the capacity for and confidence in self-expression.

In reality these categories continually overlap with each other. A single play activity often involves several types of play at any one time.

Defining play

Despite the growing interest in and study of play it is still very hard to define. Much depends on the conditions in which activities take place and the state of mind of the person doing them. An activity might be playful to one child but not to another; the same child can enjoy an activity one day and hate it the next; the same activity can be work or play depending on the situation in which it happens. There is still no single definition of play that is totally satisfactory.

The importance of play

In spite of the difficulty in being absolutely clear about what play is, there is now little doubt about the importance of its contribution to nearly all aspects of development. Current research is exploring the conditions which are best for maximising the potential benefit of play to children's development and adult involvement is now generally seen as an important enhancing factor to the quality of children's play. The main role of the adult is to provide enough stimulating opportunities for different types of play.

INDEX

First published in 1986 by Usborne Publishing Ltd, Usborne House, Saffron Hill, London
EC1N 8RT, England. Copyright © 1986 Usborne Publishing Ltd.

Printed in Spain